Arthur

EARLY ENGLISH TEXT SOCIETY

Original Series, No. 2

1864 (second edition 1869;

reprinted 1965)

PRICE 7s. 6d.

Arthur

A SHORT SKETCH OF HIS LIFE AND
HISTORY IN ENGLISH VERSE

EDITED FROM
THE MARQUIS OF BATH'S MS.
LIBER RUBEUS BATHONIÆ, 1428 A.D.

BY

FREDERICK J. FURNIVALL

Published for
THE EARLY ENGLISH TEXT SOCIETY
by the
OXFORD UNIVERSITY PRESS
LONDON   NEW YORK   TORONTO

OXFORD
UNIVERSITY PRESS

Great Clarendon Street, Oxford OX2 6DP
United Kingdom

Oxford University Press is a department of the University of Oxford.
It furthers the University's objective of excellence in research, scholarship,
and education by publishing worldwide. Oxford is a registered trade mark of
Oxford University Press in the UK and in certain other countries

© The Early English Text Society 1864

The moral rights of the authors have been asserted

Database right Oxford University Press (maker)

First Edition published in 1864
Second Edition 1869
Reprinted 1965, 1998

All rights reserved. No part of this publication may be reproduced,
stored in a retrieval system, or transmitted, in any form or by any means,
without the prior permission in writing of Oxford University Press,
or as expressly permitted by law, or under terms agreed with the appropriate
reprographics rights organization. Enquiries concerning reproduction
outside the scope of the above should be sent to the Rights Department,
Oxford University Press, at the address above

You must not circulate this book in any other form
and you must impose this same condition on any acquirer

Published in the United States of America by Oxford University Press
198 Madison Avenue, New York, NY 10016, United States of America

British Library Cataloguing in Publication Data
Data available

Library of Congress Cataloging in Publication Data
Data available

Original Series, 2
ISBN 978-0-85-991800-8

PREFACE.

As one of the chief objects of the Early English Text Society is to print every Early English Text relating to Arthur, the Committee have decided that this short sketch of the British hero's life shall form one of the first issue of the Society's publications. The six hundred and forty-two English lines here printed occur in an incomplete Latin Chronicle of the Kings of Britain, an abbreviation of the *Brut*, bound up with many other valuable pieces in the *Liber Rubeus Bathoniæ*, 1428 A.D.,[1] belonging to the Marquis of Bath. The old chronicler has dealt with Uther Pendragon, and is narrating Arthur's deeds,—telling of the siege of Bath, of Brounsteelt (Excalibur) '*caliburni, gladii Arthuri*,' of the conquest of Scotland, Ireland, Gothland, and the founding of the *Rotunda Tabula*, made round that none should be above, none below, but all sit equal—when, as if feeling that Latin prose was no fit vehicle for telling of Arthur, king of men, he breaks out into English verse,

> "Herkeneþ, þat loueþ honour,
> Of kyng Arthour & hys labour."

The story he tells is an abstract, with omissions, of the earlier version of Geoffry of Monmouth, before the love of Guinevere for Lancelot was introduced by the French-writing

---

[1] This is the date on the back of the case of the MS.

English romancers of the Lionheart's time (so far as I know), into the Arthur Tales. The fact of Mordred's being Arthur's son, begotten by him on his sister, King Lot's wife, is also omitted; so that the story is just that of a British king founding the Round Table, conquering Scotland, Ireland, Gothland, and divers parts of France, killing a giant from Spain, beating Lucius the Emperor of Rome, and returning home to lose his own life, after the battle in which the traitor whom he had trusted, and who has seized his queen and his land, was slain.

> " He that will more look,
> Read on the French book"

says our verse-writer: and to that the modern reader must still be referred, or to the translations of parts of it, which we hope to print or reprint, and that most pleasantly jumbled abstract of its parts by Sir Thomas Maleor, Knight, which has long been the delight of many a reader,—though despised by the stern old Ascham, whose Scholemaster was to turn it out of the land.—There the glory of the Holy Grail will be revealed to him; there the Knight of God made known; there the only true lovers in the world will tell their loves and kiss their kisses before him; and the Fates which of old enforced the penalty of sin will show that their arm is not shortened, and that though the brave and guilty king fights well and gathers all the glory of the world around him, yet still the sword is over his head, and, for the evil that he has done, his life and vain imaginings must pass away in dust and confusion.

Of the language of the Poem there is little to say: its dialect is mostly Southern, as shown by the verbal plural *th*, the *vyve* for five, *zyx* for six, *ych* for I, *har* (their), *ham* (them), for *her*, *hem*; *hulle*, *dude*, *ʒut*, for hill, did, yet, the infinitive in *y* *(rekeny)*, etc.; but Northern forms appear, as *fra*, from (l. 628), *at*, that (l. 640). Of its poetical merits, every reader will judge for himself; but that it has power in some parts I hope few will deny. Arthur's answer to Lucius, and two lines in the duel with Frollo,

> "There was no word y-spoke,
> But eche had other by the throte,"

are to be noted. Parts of the MS. have very much faded since it was written some ten or twenty years before 1450, so that a few of the words are queried in the print. The MS. contains a few metrical points and stops, which I have here printed between parentheses ( ). The expansions of the contractions are printed in italics, but the ordinary doubt whether the final lined *n* or *u*—for they are often undistinguishable—is to be printed n*e*, n*ne*, *u*n, or u*n*, exists here too. I have generally printed it ñ.

I am indebted to Mr Sims, of the Manuscript Department of the British Museum, for pointing out the Poem to me, and to the Marquis of Bath for his kind permission to copy it for printing.

Old Square, Lincoln's Inn,
London, W.C., August 30, 1864.
(Revised, March 2, 1869.)

ARTHUR,

FROM THE MARQUIS OF BATH'S MS.

1428 A.D.

[The Latin side-notes in italics and Clarendon, and the stops of the text in parentheses ( ), are those of the MS.]

Herkenoþ, þat loueþ honour,   [leaf 42, back]
Of kyng Arthour & hys labour;
And furst how he was bygete,   How Arthur was begotten
4 As þat we in bokis do rede.
Vther pendragoñ was hys fader,   by Pendragon on Ygerne.
And ygerne was hys Moder.
Pendragoñ ys in walysch   Pendragon (*t.i.* Dragon's Head) made two painted dragons,
8 'Dragones heed' on Englysch
He maked ypeynted dragoñs two;
Oon schold[1] byfore him goo
Whan he went to batayle,
12 Whan he wold hys foes sayle;
That other abood at wynchester,
Euer-more stylle there.
Bretones ȝaf hym þat Name,   and thence had his name.
16 Vther Pendragoñ þe same,
For þat skyle fer & nere
Euer-more hyt to bere.
¶
The Erles wyff of Cornewayle   How Uther loved the Earl of Cornwall's wife,
20 He loued to Muche sanȝ fayle;

---

[1] 'scold' over an erasure in the text; 'schold' in the left margin.

Merlyn wyþ hys sotelnesse
Turned vtheris lyknesse,
And maked hym lyche þe Erl anone,
24 And wyþ hys wyff (:) his wyll to done
In þe countre of Cornewell :
In þe Castel of Tyntagell,
Thus vther, yf y schall nat lye,

and begat Arthur in adultery.   28 Bygat Arthour in avowtrye.
Whan vther Pendragoñ was deed,

Arthur is crowned,   Arthour anon was y-crowned ;
He was courteys, large, & Gent
32 To alle puple verrament ;
Beaute, Myȝt, amyable chere
To alle Men ferre and neere ;
Hys port (;) hys ȝyftes gentyll

is loved of all,   36 Maked hym y-loved wyll ;
Ech mon was glad of hys presence,
And drade to do hym dysplesañce ;

is strong   A stronger Man of hys honde
40 was neuer founde on any londe,

and courteous.   As courteys as any Mayde :—
þus wryteþ of hym þat hym a-sayde.

[leaf 42 bk, col. 2.]   At Cayrlyoñ wythoute fable,

He makes the Round Table,   44 He let make þe Rounde table :
And why þat he maked hyt þus,
þis was þe resoun y-wyss,—

that all at it might be equal.   þat no man schulde sytt aboue other,
48 Ne haue indignacioun of hys broþer ;
And alle hadde (.)oo(.) seruyse,
For no pryde scholde aryse
For any degree of syttynge,
52 Oþer for any seruynge :
þus he kept þe table Rounde
Whyle he leuyd on þe grounde.

After his first conquests   After he hadde conquered Skotlond
56 Yrland & Gotland,

Þan leuyd he at þe best
Twelf ȝeeris on alle reste
Wyþoute werre (:) tyll at þe laste
60 He þouȝt to make (.)a(.) nywe conqueste.
Into Fraunce wyþ gode counceyle
he wolde weende (:) & hyt assayle,
þat Rome þo kept vnder Myght,
64 Vnder Frollo (:) a worthy knyght
þat fraunce hadde þo to kepe,
To rywle, defende, & to lede.
Arthour and Frollo fowȝt in feld ;
68 þere deyde many vnder scheld.
Frollo in-to Paryss fly,
Wyth strenkthe kept hyt wysely :
Arthour byseged þat Syte & town
72 Tyll þeire vytayl was y-doon.
Frollo þat worthy knyght
Proferyd wyth Arthour for to fyght
Vnder þis wyse & condicioun,—
76 " Ho hadde þe Maystrie (:) haue þe crown ;
And no mo men but þey two."
Þe day was sett (:) to-geder þey go :
Fayr hyt was to byholde
80 In suche two knyȝhteȝ bolde :
Þer was no word y-spoke,
But eche hadde other by þe þrote ;
Þey smote wyth trounchoun & wyth swerd ;'
84 þat hyt seye, were a-ferd ;
Frollo fowȝt wyþ hys ax (:) as men dude se ;
He hytt Arthour (:) so sore (:) þat he felle on kne.
He ros vp raply (:) and smot hym full sore ;
88 He dude hym to grent a (.) soueȝ[1] þerfore.
Thus they hyw on helmes hye,
And schatered on wyþ scheldes.
Þe puple by-gan to crye
92 þat stood on þe feldes ;

he lives twelve years in peace,

and then invades France.

He beats Frollo back to Paris,

and there besieges him, till.

Frollo challenges him to single combat.

They fight :

[leaf 43.]
(Frollo with his axe)

[1 ? soneȝ]

Ther ne wyst no man, as y can lere,
Who of ham two was þe bettere þere.

till Arthur in wrath takes Brownsteel,

Arthour was chafed & wexed wroth,
96 He hente brounsteell / and to Frollo goth;

Caliburnus Arthuri Gladius [with a sketch thereof in the MS.] *and strikes Frollo dead.*

Brounstell was heuy & also kene;
Fram þe schulder (:) to þe syde went bytwene
Off frollo / and þan he fell to þe grounde
100 Ryȝt as he moste / deed (.) in lyte stounde.
Frensch men made doell & wept full faste;
þeir Crowne of fraunce þere þey loste.

Arthur takes Paris.

Than wente Arthour in-to paryse
104 And toke þe castell & þe town at hys avyse.

Glory to God.

Worschuped be god of hys grete grace
þat þus ȝeueþ fortune (:) and worschup to þe Reme;
Thanke ȝe hym all þat beþ on þis place,

Say ye a Pater Noster therefore.

108 And seyeþ a Pater noster wythout any Beeme.
¶   // Pater noster. //

Arthour fram Paryse went wyth hys Rowte,

Arthur conquers the countries around,

And conquered þe Coñtre on euery syde aboute;
Angeoy,¹ Peytow, Berry, & Gaskoyne,
112 Nauerne, Burgoñ / Loreyn & Toreyne;
He daunted þe proude / & hawted þe poure;
He dwelt long in Paryss after in honoure;
He was drad and loued in coñtreis abowte;
116 Heyest & lowest hym Loved & alowte;
And vp-on an Estour tyme sone afterward

distributes them among his knights,

He fested hys knyghtis & ȝaf ham gret reward;
To hys Styward he ȝaf Angers & Añgeye;
120 To Bedewer hys botyler he ȝaf Normandye;
He ȝaf to Holdyne flaundrys parde;
To Borel hys Cosyn, Boloyne þe Cyte;
And eche man, after þe astat þat he was,
124 He rewarded hem alle, boþe More & lasse,
And ȝaf hem reward, boþe lond and Fee,

and returns to Britain.

And turned to Breteyn, to Carlyoñ ayhe.

¹ ? MS. perhaps *Angecye*. See *Angeoy*, l. 312.

Arthour wolde of honour
128 Hold a fest at Eestour
　　Of regalye & worthynesse,
　　And feede alle hys frendess ;
　　And sende Messanger
132 To kynges ferre & neer
　　þat were to hym Omager,
　　to come to þis Dyner.
　　And alle at oo certeyn day
136 They come þyder in gode aray,
　　And kept þeire Ceson
　　At þe Castell Carlyon.
　　Thys fest was Muche Moore
140 þan euere Arthour made a-fore ;
　　For þere was Vrweyn þe kynge
　　Of scottes at þat dynynge,
　　Stater þe kyng of south wales,
144 Cadwell þe kyng of north waleȝ,
　　Gwylmar þe kyng of yrland,
　　Dolmad þe kyng of guthland,
　　Malgan of yselond also,
148 Archyl of Denmarch þerto,
　　Aloth þe kyng of Norwey,
　　Souenas þe kyng of Orkenye,
　　Of Breteyn þe kyng Hoel,
152 Cador Erl of Cornewell,
　　Morice þe Erl of Gloucestre,
　　Marran Erl of Wynchestre,
　　Gwergound Erl of herford,
156 Booȝ Erl of Oxenford,
　　Of bathe vngent þe Erl also,
　　Cursal of Chestre þer-to,
　　Euerad Erl of Salesbury,[1]
160 Kynmar Erl of Canterbury,
　　Ionas þe Erl of Dorcestre,

Arthur gives an Easter Feast

at Carlyon, greater than ere before.

Ten kings were there,

and thirteen earls

(including him of Bath),

[1] The *s* is rubbed : the word may be "onlesbury."

Valence þe Erl of Sylchestre,
Iugeyn of Leyccer [?] þerto,
164 Argal of warwyk also,—
Kynges & Erles Echon
þes were; & many anoþer goom
Gret of astaat, & þe beste,
168 þes were at þe Feste.
Other also gentyls grete
Were þere at þat Meete,
Sauer appon Donand,
172 Regeym & Alard,
Reyneʒ fitʒ Colys,
Tadeus fitʒ Reis,
Delyn fitʒ Dauid,
176 Kymbelyn le fitʒ Gryffith,
Gryffitʒ þe sone of Nagand,
þes were þere also theoband:
Alle þes were þere wythoute fable,
180 Wythoute ham of þe rounde table.
Thre archebusschopes þer were also,
And other busschopes many mo—
Aħ þis mayne were nat al-oone;
184 Wyth ham com many a Goome.
þis feste dured dayes þre
In reueħ & solempnite.
Of byʒonde þe See also
188 Many lordeʒ were þere þo.
Now resteþ alle wyþ Me,
And say a Pater & Aue.
¶ Pater noster.
The þrydde day folowyng
192 Then coom nywe tydynge,
þe whyle þey sete at þe Mete
Messagers were In ylete;
Weħ arayd forsoþe þey come,
196 Y-send fram cite of Rome

Wyþ lettres of þe Emperoures
Whas name was Lucies.
þes lettres were opened & vnfold,
200 And þe tydyng' to alle men told,
Whas sentence, yf y ne lye,
Was after þat y can aspye :
¶ Lucius þe grete Emperour
204 To hys Enemy Arthour :—
We woñdereþ of þi wodeness
And also of þy Madnesse !
How darst þow any wyse
208 Aȝenst the Emperour þus aryse,
And ryde on Remes on eche wey,
And make kyngeȝ to þe obey ?
þu art wood on þe Nolle !
212 þu hast Scley owre cosyn frolle ;
þu schalt be tawȝt at a schort day
for to make such aray.
Oure cosyn Iulius cesar
216 Somme tyme conquered þar ;
To Rome þu owest hys trybut ;
We chargeþ þe to paye vs hyt.
Thy pryde we woll alaye
220 þat makest so gret aray :
We commandeþ þe on haste
To paye owre trybut faste ;
þu hast scley frolle in fraunce
224 þat hadde vnder vs þere gouernaunce,
And wyþholdest oure tribute þerto :
þu schalt be tawȝt þu hast mysdo :
We commandeþ þe in haste soone
228 þat þu come to vs at Rome
To vnderfang oure ordynaunce
For þy dysobediaunce ;
As þu wold nat leȝe þy lyf,
232 Fulfylle þys wythoute stryff."
(¶ . . . . . ¶ . . . . . ¶ . . . . . ¶)

*Luci*us.

L*ite*ra Lucii
imperat*or*is.

saying, that to
have invaded
France, etc., and
made kings,
Arthur must be
mad in his noll ;

[leaf 44, col. 1.]

that he must pay
his tribute,

and come to
Rome to be pun-
ished for his dis-
obedience.

¶ Whan þis lettre was open & rad,
þe bretoñs & aƚƚ men were mad,
And wolde þe messager scle :—
236 "Nay," seyd Arthour, "per de,
That were aȝenst aƚƚ kynde,
A messager to bete or bynde ;
Y charge alle men here
240 For to make ham good chere."
And after Mete sanȝ fayl
Wyþ hys lordes he hadde counsayl ;
And alle asented þer-to,
244 Arthour to Rome scholde go ;
And þey ne wolde in hys trauayle
Wyþ strenkþ & good neuer fayle.
Than Arthour wroot to Rome a lettre,
248 Was sentence was somm-what byttere,
And seyde in þis manere
As ȝe may hure here :—

"KNoweþ weƚƚ ȝe of Romayne,
252 Y am kyng Arthour of Bretayne.
Frañce, y haue conquered hyt,
Y schaƚƚ defende & kepe hyt ȝut,
Y come to Rome, as y am tryw,
256 To take my trybut (.) to me dywe,
But noon þere for to paye,
By my werk ȝe schaƚƚ asay ;
For þe Emperour Constantyne
260 þat was þe Soone of Elyne,
þat was a Bretoñ of þis lond,
Conquered Rome wyth hys hond,
And so ȝe oweþ me tribut :
264 Y charge ȝow þat ȝe pay me hyt.
¶
Also Maximian kyng of Bretaingne
Co[n]quered al frañce & Almayne,
Lombardye, Rome, & ytalye—

268 By ȝoure bokis ȝe may a-spye.
Y am þeir Eyr & þeyre lynage,
Y aske ȝow my trywage."

Þis lettre was celyd fast,
272 Y-take the Messagereȝ on hast;
Arthour ȝaf ham ȝyfteȝ grete,
And chered ham wyþ drynk and Mete.   *Lucius's messengers return to him,*
Þey hasted ham to come hoom;
276 Byfor þe Emperour þey beþ coom;
Saluted hym as resoñ ys,
And toke hym þes letterys.
Þey seyde to þe Emperour
280 "We have be wyþ kyng Arthour;
But such anoþer as he ys oon,
Say neuer no Man.
He ys serued on hys howshold
284 Wyþ kynges, Erles, worthy & bold;
Hys worthynesse, sur Emperour,
Passeþ Much aff ȝowre;
He seyde he wolde hyder come   *and give him Arthur's message.*
288 And take trywage of aff Rome,
We dowteþ last he wol do soo,
For he ys Myghty ynow þer-too."
Now, erst þan we goo ferþer,
292 Every man þat ys here
Sey a Pater noster
And ave wyþ gode chere.   Amen.

¶   Pater noster
       Abe Maria.

Now stureth hym self Arthour   *[leaf 44, back.]*
296 Þenkyng on hys labour,   *Arthur prepares for his expedition to Rome.*
And gaderyþ to hym strenghth aboute,
Hys kynges & Erles on a rowte—
A fayr syȝt to Mannes ye
300 To see such a cheualrye,—

Has five kings,	The kyng of Gotland,
	Also þe kyng of Irland,
	The kyng of ysland / & of Orkenye,
	304 þis was worthy Maynye;
	The kyng of Denmark also was þere,
	þis was a worthy chere:
	Eche of þese vyve at her venyw
	308 Brouȝt zyx þousand at har retenyw;
with 30,000 men,	xxx^{ti} þowsand, ych vnderstand,
	þes vyf kyngis hadde on honde.
80,000 Normans and	Than hadde he out of Normandye,
	312 Of Angeoy & of Almanye,
	Boloyne (.) Peytow & flaundres
	Fowre skore þowsand harneys—
12,000 from Chartres,	Geryn of Charteȝ .xij. þowsand
	316 þat went wyþ Artour euer at honde;
10,000 Bretons,	Hoel of bretayn, þowsandeȝ ten
	Of hardy & well fyghtyng Men;
	Out of Bretaygne hys owne land
and 40,000 British:	320 He passed fourty þowsand
	Of Archerys & off Arblastere
	þat Cowþ well þe craft of werre.
	¶ In Foot other Many a Man Moo
	324 Able to feyghte (:) as well as þo:
in all 200,000.	Two hunderd þousand
	Went wyþ hym out of lond,
	And Many moo sykerly
	328 That y can nat nombrye.
	Arthour toke þan þe lond
Britain is left in Mordred's charge.	To Moddredes owne hond;
	He kept al oþer þyng
	332 Saue þe Corowne weryng;
	But he was [fals] of hys kepynge,
	As ȝe schall hure here folewynge.
Arthur ships at Southampton,	Now than ys Artour y-Come,
	336 And hys Ost, to Sowthamptone:

THE GIANT THAT RAVISHED FAIR ELAYNE. 11

Ther was Many a Man of Myghte   ¶ Ascende*bat* naue*m* suа*m* Hamptonie.
Strong & bold also to fyghte.
Eche man hath take his schuppynge,   [leaf 44 bk, col. 2.]
340 And ys at hys loghynge.
Vp goþ þe sayl (:) þey saleþ faste :
Arthour owt of syȝt ys paste.
þe ferst lond þat he gan Meete,
344 Forsoþ hyt was Bareflete ;   and lands at Barfleet.
Ther he gan vp furst aryve.
Now well Mote Arthour spede & thryve !
And þat hys saule spede þe better,   God speed him !
348 Lat eche man sey a pater noster.

    ¶   𝔓ater noster.

Now god spede Artour well !
Hym ys comyng a nyw batell.   A new foe appears, a Spanish Giant,
Ther coom a gyant out of spayne,
352 And rauasched had fayr Elayne ;
He had brouȝt heor' vp on an hulle—
Mornyng hyt ys to hure or telle—
Cosyn heo was to kyng Hoell,
356 A damesel fayr and gentell ;
And ȝut ferþermore to,
He rauasched heore Moder also.   who has slain fair Elayne.
He dude þe damesel for to dye,
360 For he myght not lygge heor' bye.
Whan þis was told to Artour,
He maked Much dolour,
And send Bedewer for to spye   Arthur sends Bedwere first as a spy,
364 How he myght come hym bye ;
And he was nat Sclowh,
But to þe hulle hym drowh
þat Closed was wyþ water stronge,
368 þe hulle a-Mydde gret & longe ;
He went ouer to þe hulle syde,
And þere a fonde a womman byde,
þat sorwedd & wept Mornynge

ARTHUR'S FIGHT WITH THE GIANT.

<small>and then (with Bedwere and Key) starts on his adventure.</small>

<small>[¹ *by* in a later hand, above.]</small>

<small>He kills the Giant,</small>

<small>whose horrible head is shown to the host,</small>

<small>and St. Mary's Chapel is built in honour of the victory.</small>

<small>News of Lucius's approach is brought,</small>

372 For Eleynes deþ & departynge,
And bad Bedewer to fle also
Last he were ded more to;
" For yf þe Gyant fynde þe,
376 Wythoute dowte he wyll þe sclc."
Bedwer wyþ all hastynge
Tolde Arthour all þis þynge.
Amorwe whan þat hyt was day
380 Arthour toke þyder hys way,   [leaf 45]
Bedewer wyþ hym wente, & keye,—
Men þat cowþe well þe weye,—
And broute Arthour Meyntenañt
384 Euen ¹ byfore þe gyant.
Arthour fowȝt wyþ þat wyght;
He had almost ylost hys Myght:
Wyþ Muche peyne, þruȝ goddeȝ grace
388 He sclowh þe Geant in þat place,
And þan he made Bedewere
To smyte of hys heed þere.
To þe Ost he dude hyt brynge,
392 And þeron was gret woñdrynge,
Hyt was so oryble & so greet,
More þan any Horse heed.
Than hadde hoel Ioye ynowh
396 For þat Arthour so hym sclowh;
And for a perpetuel Memorie
He Made a chapell of seynt Marye
In þe hulle vpon þe pleyne,
400 Wyþ-Inne þat (:) þe tumbe of Eleyne;   tombe.
And þat name wyþoute nay
Hyt bereþ ȝut in-to þis day.
Now ys an ende of þis þynge,
404 And artour haþ nyw tydynge:
Lucy þe Emperour wyþ hys host
Comeþ fast in gret bost;
þey helyþ ouer all þe lond,

408 Fowre hunderd þowsand *with an army of 400,124 men.*
 An hunderd & foure & twenty,—
 Thus herawdes dude ham rekeny;—
 Thus he hadde gadered to hym
412 Of cristiens and of Sarasyn,
 Wyþ aℓℓ hys wytt & labour
 To destroyen Arthour.
 Arthour dude wyselye,
416 And hadde euer gode aspye
 Of lucyes gouernynge
 And of hys þyder comynge;
 But somme seyde hyt were folye *Some advise Arthur to turn and flee,*
420 To fyght aȝenst Emperour lucie,
 For he hadde sexe[1] euere aȝenst oon,
 & counceyled Arthour to fle & goon.
 Wyþ þe Emperour come kynges Many oon, *[leaf 45, col. 2.]*
424 And aℓℓ þeire power hooℓℓ & soom;
 Stronger men Myȝt no man see,
 As fuℓℓ of drede as þey myght be;
 But / Arthour was nat dysmayd,
428 He tryst on god, & was wel payd, *but he trusts in God,*
 And prayd þe hye trynyte
 Euer hys help forto be;
 And aℓℓ hys Men wyþ oo voyse
432 Cryede to god wyþ Oo noyse,
 "Fader in heuene, þy wyℓℓ be doon; *to whom his soldiers pray*
 Defende þy puple fram þeire foon,
 And lat nat þe heþoñ Men
436 Destroye þe puple crystien:
 Haue Mercy on þy se[r]uañtis bonde,
 And kepe ham fram þe heþoñ honde; *to keep them from the heathen's hands.*

[1] I read this *sepe* before; but now I read it *sexe*; for though the *x* is not like that of *ax*, l. 85, or of *axes*, l. 463, Maxymyan, 507, next 508, Saxoynes, 521, &c., yet it is something like that of the 'Xristianitas durat' of the headlines of the English pages, and the 'Destructio xrianitatis' of the headline on the back of leaf 46, and Sexaginta, leaf 66, back. But as Arthur had 200,000, and Lucius only 400,124, *sexe* should be *two*.

þe Muchelnesse of Men sainfayle
440 Ys nat victorie in Batayle ;
But after þe wyll þat in heuene ys,
So þe victorie falleþ y-wys."

Arthur's "For-
ward!"
Than seyd Arthour, "hyt ys so :
444 Auant Baner, & be Goo."
Now frendes all, for goddes loue,
Rereþ ȝowre hertes to god aboue,
And seyeþ ȝowre prayeris faste,
448 þat we well spede furst & laste.

¶ Pater noster.

The emperour tryst on hys men,
And þat haþ bygyled hym ;
Forsothe hyt most nedeȝ be so,

Maledictus qui
confidet in
homine.
452 For þey beþ cursed þat well hyt do,
Such all myght comeþ of god ;
To tryst on hym, y hold hyt good,
Lucye haþ pyght his pauelon
456 And sprad wyþ pryde his gunfanon ;
His claryons blastes full grete blywe,

The battle be-
gins.
Archeris schot (:) Men ouer-thrywe ;
Bowes, arwes, & arblastere
460 Schot sore all y-vere ;
Quarels, arwes, þey fly smerte ;
þe fyched Men þruȝ heed & herte ;
Axes, sperys, and gysarmes gret,
464 Clefte Many a prowt Mannes heed :
Hors & steedes gan to grent,
And deyde wyþ strokis þat þey hente ;

[leaf 45, back.]
Many a man þere lost hys lyf,
468 Many on was wedyw þat was wyff ;

Men are wetshod
with brains and
blood.
þere men were wetschoede
All of Brayn & of blode ;
Gret rywth hyt was to seyn
472 þe feltes full of men y-scleyn ;

Lucius is slain,
Lucy þe Emperour also was dede ;

But ho hym sclowh, y can nat rede;
He, for aᛚ hys grete Renoun,   *not able to stand against Arthur.*
476 Aʒenst Arthour hadde no fusoun,
No more þan haue twenty schep
Aʒenst vyve wolfeʒ greet.
To god be euere alle honoureʒ!
480 The falde was hys & Arthoureʒ.
Arthour, as he scholde done,   *Arthur sends Lucius's body to Rome,*
Sende lucyes body to Rome.
Whan þe Romeynes say þis,
484 þo þey dradde Arthour & hys.
Also he buryed Bedewere   *buries Bedwere and others*
Hys frend and / hys Botyler,
And so he dude other Echon
488 In Abbeys of Relygyoñ   *in Abbeys,*
þat were cristien of name;
He dude to alle þe same;
And dude for ham Masse synge
492 Wyth solempne song & offrynge,
And bood þere for to rest
Tyᛚ þat wynter was past,   *and stays the winter,*
Boþe he (.) hys Men echone
496 Seruyd god in deuocione,
þankyng god of hys Myʒt   *thanking God*
þat kepeþ hys seruauntez ryʒt,
And suffreþ noon for to spylle
500 þat hym loueþ & tryste wylle:
þus worschup god dude certeyn   *for His honour to England.*
To Englond, þat þo was Bretayn;   [*Of the difference between More (or Great) Britain, and Little Britain.*]
þe More Breteyn Englond ys—
504 As men may rede on Cronyclys—
Byʒend þe See Bretayne þer ys,
þat haþ hys name forsoþe of þis,
For þe kyng Maxymyan,—   *Quomodo anglia est Britannia maior, & quare maior*
508 þe next after Octauyan,—
He conquered aᛚ Armoryk,   [lf. 45 bk, col. 2.]

And to þe Reme named hyt lyk :
Amorica on latyn me cleped þat lond,
512 Tyl Maxymyan co[n]queryd hyt wyth honde,
And called hyt lyte bretayne þan,
So hyʒt þis lond þat he coom fram ;
For perpetuell Mynde of grete Bretayne
516 He called hyt lyte Bretayne,
þat Men schulde kepe in Mynde & wytt
How þis lond conqueryd hytt ;
For Walsch Men beþ Bretouns of kynde—
520 Know þat well fast on Mynde—
Englysch men beþ Saxoynes,
þat beþ of Engistes Soones ;
There-fore þe walsch man Bretoñ
524 Seyþ & clepeþ vs "Sayson" *Þat ys to seye vpon a reess, "Stynkyng Saxone, be on pees."*
And seyþ (.) " taw or (.) Peyd Saysen brou*n*t " [1]
Whan he ys wroth (:) or ellys dro*u*nke ;
Hauyng Mynde of Engystis Men
528 þat wyth gyle sclow þeyre kyn :
At þe place of þe Stonehenge
ʒut þey þenkeþ for to venge :
And þàt hyt neuere be so,
532 Seyþ a Pater noster more to.

¶   **Pater noster.**

Now turne we to oure labour,
And lat vs speke of Arthour :
He cast on herte sone
536 After þat to go to Rome,
And spak of Passage & hys wey
Forth ouer Moñt Ioye.
And sone after vpon an owr
540 He hurde of Mordred the tretour

---

[1] Pughe's abridged Dictionary gives *tau*, *v.a.* be still ; *taw*, *s.m.* and *adj.* quiet, silence, silent ; *paid*, *s.m.* a cessation, quiet ; *bront*, *a.* nasty, filthy, surly. *Or*, says Dr. Benj. Davies, you must take as equal to the modern Welsh *wr*, man, if it is not English ; *peyd* is cease, pause ; *taw*, be silent.

OF MORDRED'S TREACHERY AND ARTHUR'S RETURN.

  That hadde all þis lond on warde—
  Euyll moot such fare, and harde!
  Who may best bygyle a man
544 But such as he tryst vpan?
  Þer ys no man wel nye, y tryste,
  Þat can be waar of hadde wyste.—
  Mordred, þis falss Man,
548 Much sorw þo bygan;
  He stuffed alle castells
  Wyþ armyre & vytells,
  And strenghthed hym on eche syde
552 Wyth Men of contreys ferre & wyde: [leaf 46.]
  He toke þe qweene, Arthourez wyff, how the traitor had seized the
  Aȝenst goddes lawe & gode lyff, queen, his (Arthur's) wife,
  And putte heore to soiourne þo
556 At Euerwyk (:) god ȝyf hym wo.—
  Yhork ys Euerwyk (:) and put her at York.
  & so me calleþ hyt.—
  Arthour aryved at Whytsond Arthur then comes home,
560 Wyth gret Myght & strong hond,
  And Mordred sainȝ fayl fights Mordred,
  Ȝaf hym þo a strong batayl;
  Many a man, as y rede,
564 þat day was þere dede;
  Arthoures nevew Waweyn
  þat day was þere y-sclayn, and Gawain is slain.
  And oþer knyȝtes Many moo:
568 Þan Arthour was heuy & woo.
  Mordred fly toward Londoun; Mordred flies to London,
  He most nat come in þe toun:
  Þan fled he to Wynchester
572 And wyth hys Mayne kep hym þer';
  And Arthour on gret haste
  Pursywed after hym faste.
  Mordred wythoute fayle
576 Fled in-to Cornewayle. and then to Cornwall.

    D

The qwene wyþoute lesyng
Hurde of þis tydyng,
And how Mordred was flow,
580 And how to Cornewale he hym drow.
Heo of Mercy hadde noon hoope,
Ther-for he dude on a Russet cote,

The Queen turns nun at Carlyon.

And to Carlyoñ ys preuyly Roñne,
584 And made heore self þo a Noñne;
Fro þat place neuer heo wende,
But of heore lyf þere made an ende.

Gawain

Waweynes body, as y reede,
588 And other lordes þat weere deede,

is buried in Scotland.

Arthour sente in-to skotlonde,
And buryed ham þere, y vnderstonde.
Muche folke þerhenne he toke þo,

Northern men and others come to Arthur.

592 Of Northumber-lond also
Fram dyverse places to Arthour come
Hys wyll to werk & to done :
Thus he sembled a full gret Ost;
596 To Cornewayle he draweþ hym fast
After þat Mordred þe traytour
þat hadde do hym Much dyshonour.

[leaf 46, col. 2.]

That tretour hadde gret Strength
600 And fulled þat lond on brede & length,

He gives Mordred battle.

Such a batell as þere was redy þo
Hadde neuer Arthour byfore y-doo :
They fowȝt tyl þer come doun bloode

Bellum arthuri apud Camelertonum in Cornubia.

604 As a(.) Ryver or (.)a(.) flood;
þey fowȝt euer sore & sadde ;
Men nyst ho þe betere hadde ;
But at þe last Certeyn

Mordred is slain,

608 Was Mordred & alle hys y-sclayn;

Arthur wounded,

And Arthour y-bete wyþ wounde,
He Myght not stonde on grounde;

and carried to Avelon, or Auelona .i. insula pomorum Glastonia.

But on lyter ryȝt anon
612 Was browȝt to Aueloñ

þat was a place fayr & Mury ;
Now hyt hooteþ Glastyngbury. *Glastonbury,*
Ther Arthour þat worthy kyng *where he dies,*
616 Maked hys lyues endyng ;
But for he skaped þat batell y-wys,
Bretoñs & Cornysch seyeþ þus,
" þat he leuyth ȝut parde,
620 And schall come & be a kyng aȝe."
At glastyngbury on þe qweer
þey made Artoureȝ toumbe þere, *and is buried,*
And wrote wyth latyn vers þus, *A.D. 542.*
624 Hic iacet Arthurus, rex quondam, rex que futurus.
Thys was þus forsoþe ydone
þe yheer after þe Incarnacione, *Anno domini*
Vyf hundred (.) fourty & two. *quingentesimo quadragesimo secundo.*
628 Now saue vs alle fra woo
Ihesu cryst, heuenly kyng,
& graunt vs alle hys blessyng ;
And þat hyt Moote so be,
632 Seyeþ alle Pater & Aue.
¶ 𝔓ater noster / 𝔄ue /
Ho þat woll more loke,
Reed on þe frensch boke, *Read the French Book for the rest.*
And he schall fynde þere
636 þynges þat y leete here.
But yf þat god wolle graunte grace,
y schall rehercy in þis place
Alle þe kyngez þat after were,
640 And what names at þey bere ;
And ho þat woll þeyre gestes loke,
Reed on þe Frensch boke.   Amen fiat.

[On the back of leaf 46 follows : ' Destructio christianitatis /
Et reformàcio eiusdem. Constantinus. Post Arthurum
regnauit Constantinus, filius Cador, Comitis Cornubie,
nepos Arthuri / iste constantinus interfecit duos filios
Mordredi spurios, qui Mouerunt bellum contra eum
propter patrem eorum,' &c., &c.]

WORDS.

a, he, l. 370.
alowte, l. 116, bowed down to.
aspye, *sb.* espial, l. 416; *vb.* ascertain, ll. 202, 268.
ayhe, again, l. 126.
beeme, *sb.* ? noise, display, from A.S. *béme,* a trumpet, l. 108.
doelle, l. 101, sorrow.
falde, l. 480, felt, l. 472; field.
foon, l. 434, foes.
fusoun, gain, victory, l. 476. L. *fusio,* outpouring, plenty; common in Scotland for 'pith, bottom.'
fyched, pierced, l. 462.
goom, man, l. 166.
gysarme, l. 463. *Hallebarde, pique, hache.* Roquefort.
hadde wyste, l. 546, had I known (how it would have turned out). See Nares, and the Poem "Beware of had-I-wyst," that he quotes. "Beware of *had-I-wyst,* whose fine bringes care and smart."
hawted, exalted, l. 113.
he, she, l. 582.
heo, l. 581, she.
helyth, cover (or pour out, *helè* Wilts., *hale* Dorset.), l. 407.
hente, l. 96, took; l. 466, received.
hulle, l. 399, hill.
last, lest, l. 289.
leete, l. 636, leave, omit.
loghynge, lodging, l. 344.
lynage, descendant, l. 269.
meyntenaunt, l. 383, presently, soon.

muchelnesse, *sb.* muchness, number and power, l. 439.
mynde, remembrance, l. 527.
nyst, l. 606, ne wyst, knew not.
oo, one, l. 49, 135.
pyght, l. 455, pitched.
raply, l. 87, quickly.
rees, l. 524, rush, stir?
remes, l. 209, realms.
sayle, assail, attack, l. 12.
scley, slain, l. 212.
skyle, *sb.* reason, l. 17.
soueȝ (?), sough, moan, l. 88.
that, ye who, l. 1; those who, l. 42, 84.
theoband (l. 178), is, I expect, miswritten for theo*d*and; A.S. *þeodan,* to join; *ge-þeod-an,* to join, associate.
therhenne, thence, l. 591.
tho, l. 138, then.
toke, gave, l. 329.
trywage, l. 270, 288, truage, tribute.
venge, have revenge, take vengeance, l. 530.
verrament, truly, l. 32.
was, whose, l. 248.
whas, whose, l. 198, 201.
wocd, wild, mad, l. 211.
ydoon, done, spent, l. 72.
ye, l. 299, eye.
ylete, let, l. 194.
ytake, taken to, given to, l. 272.
y-vere, together, l. 460.
ywyss, certainly, l. 46.

The manufacturer's authorised representative in the EU for product safety is Oxford University Press España S.A. of El Parque Empresarial San Fernando de Henares, Avenida de Castilla, 2 - 28830 Madrid (www.oup.es/en or product.safety@oup.com). OUP España S.A. also acts as importer into Spain of products made by the manufacturer.
Printed and bound by CPI Group (UK) Ltd, Croydon, CR0 4YY

09/04/2026

02086649-0001